TO HAMISH –

WITH LOVE FROM –

GRANDMA & GRANDAD

29 MAY 2000

See if you can find this waiter
in every picture!

# OUR CRUISE

by Mike Applebee

PAVILION

For Jake, Sam, Kizzie
and, of course, Grandma

First published in Great Britain in 1993 by
PAVILION BOOKS LIMITED
26 Upper Ground, London SE1 9PD
Text and illustrations copyright © Mike Applebee 1993

The moral right of the author has been asserted.

Designed by Bet Ayer

A CIP catalogue record for this book
is available from the British Library.

ISBN  1  85793  0940

Printed and bound in Singapore by Imago

2  4  6  8  10  9  7  5  3  1

This book may be ordered by post
direct from the publisher. Please contact
the Marketing Department.
But try your bookshop first.

Hello! It's very nice to be back home, and we've got
so much to tell you about what we've been doing
on that big ship.

After we boarded the ship, we were shown to our bedroom. This was called a cabin, and some of the cabins have round windows called portholes.

Every passenger had to learn the life-jacket drill, just
in case of an emergency.

The ship had many restaurants, and all the food was delicious. These smart men called waiters served us, and we didn't have to do any washing-up!

Sometimes we went for a swim in one of the pools.
It felt very strange swimming in a pool that was on a
ship, sailing across the sea.

There were several big parties for the passengers and crew, and they were great fun. Once or twice we even went in fancy dress.

We had a great time in the casino too, but don't tell your mum and dad!

It was very exciting when there was a storm or the sea was rough. At times like this it was difficult to stay standing up.

Sometimes we spent all evening dancing, and when it was warm we would go on deck and dance in the moonlight.

We went to the ship's cinema to see some films, though the seats were so comfortable we nearly fell asleep.

If we wanted to, we could keep fit in the ship's gymnasium.

On one of the decks we could even play tennis or practise our golf.

There was also a library on board where you could borrow books, read newspapers or just go for some peace and quiet.

When we docked at foreign ports, we could get off the ship and go exploring. There were lots of things to see, and lots of time to buy presents.

We had a lovely time with plenty of fun and food and friends, and much more. It was a very special holiday, and we will always remember it.